# Problem Pages
# 11 to 16

## A Book of Mathematical Problems for

## Lower Secondary School Pupils

MATHEMATICAL ASSOCIATION

supporting mathematics in education

First published in 2003 by
The Mathematical Association
259 London Road
Leicester  LE2 3BE
United Kingdom

ISBN  0 906588 52 9


Printed and bound in Great Britain at
J. W. Arrowsmith Ltd, Bristol.

Typeset by Bill Richardson

# Introduction

This is a book of over sixty problems, together with suggested solutions. The problems are all accessible to pupils in secondary schools, although many can be solved by pupils at primary level.

The problems can be used in a variety of ways. A method which has been tried successfully is to post up a problem each week in the classroom and invite students to work on it in their own time. Working together and discussing the problems should certainly be encouraged. The suggested solution can be posted up the following week, together with a new problem. Students' solutions can be displayed and alternative, correct solutions can be a rich source of discussion. Many of the problems have a link to the standard curriculum, so they can be incorporated as an enhancement of normal teaching. The problems could form the basis of a student competition.

On the contents page, each problem is given a level of difficulty ranging from 1 to 3, which is harder. The problems are not presented in order of difficulty and are suitable for use in any order. Any difficulty rating is, inevitably, subjective and users may well disagree with some of our judgements.

It is intended that the problems and solutions should be photocopied to allow their use to be as flexible as possible. Permission is given by The Mathematical Association for purchasers to make photocopies for use in their institutions.

# Acknowledgements

This book of problems complements the earlier publication *Problem Pages* by the A and AS level subcommittee of the Teaching Committee of The Mathematical Association, which was aimed primarily at students on AS/A level or Scottish Higher courses.

Our thanks go to Doug French and Charlie Stripp for help given in suggesting problems and checking solutions.

Other publications by this group include:

*PIG and Other Tales*, a book of mathematical readings with questions, suitable for sixth fomers.

*Are You Sure? – Learning about Proof*, a book of ideas for teachers of upper secondary school students.

*Problem Pages*, a book of mathematical problems for upper secondary school students.

# Contents

| No | Title | Level | Topics |
|---|---|---|---|
| 22 | Can You Solve It? | 2 | Simultaneous Equations |
| 23 | Square Root | 2 | Square Roots, Multiplication |
| 24 | Find the Difference | 1 | Area |
| 25 | Cows | 1 | Addition |
| 26 | Prove It | 3 | Circles, Triangles |
| 27 | Adding It Up | 1 | Addition |
| 28 | Fun with Factorials | 2 | Factorials |
| 29 | How Big? | 2 | Area of Triangles |
| 30 | A Magic Hexagon | 1 | Addition |
| 31 | Why Does It Happen? | 2 | Algebra, brackets |
| 32 | Eighty One | 1 | Addition |
| 33 | Noughts and Crosses | 2 | 3-D space |
| 34 | Chess Board Problem | 3+ | Combinations |
| 35 | Feed the Fly! | 3 | Volume, Pythagoras |
| 36 | Make a Million | 1 | Prime factors |
| 37 | CD space | 2 | Circles, Pythagoras |
| 38 | Pentagon Pieces | 3 | Areas |
| 39 | A Question of Algebra | 2 | Simultaneous Equations |
| 40 | School Run | 1 | Combinations |
| 41 | An Angular Question | 2 | Combinations, Angles |
| 42 | Ring the Changes | 2 | Arrangements |

# Problem

## *The Gambler*

Big Spender, the gambler has lost his fortune of one million pounds over recent years. Every day he started with £1000 but lost it all in play.

A)   If he started playing on January 1st, 1999, what was the date when he ran out of money?

B)   If he had wanted his money to last until 1st January, 2004, about how much should he have spent each day?

# Solution

## *The Gambler*

A) He spends for 1000 days (why?) which, from January 1st 1999, includes a leap year so covers 2 years and 269 days. This takes us to September 26th, 2001.

B) Now he needs the money to last 1826 days so (why?) he must lose no more than about £547 a day (why?).

---

Big Spender, the gambler has lost his fortune of one million pounds over recent years. Every day he started with £1000 but lost it all in play.

A) If he started playing on January 1st, 1999, what was the date when he ran out of money?

B) If he had wanted his money to last until 1st January, 2004, about how much should he have spent each day?

---

*Solution No 1*

# Problem

## *Page numbers*

A new book was printed and the pages were numbered in the usual way. When these numbers were looked at it was noticed that a total of 555 digits had been used.

A)   How many pages were there in the book?

B)   How many fives were used?

C)   If all the digits used were added up, what would the total be?

# Solution

## *Page Numbers*

A)  Pages 1 to 9 use 9 digits, then 10 to 99 use 180 digits so there are **122** more pages (with 3 digits each). This means the book has 221 pages altogether.

B)  There are 22 fives used in the units of these pages and 10 in each of the fifties and one hundred and fifties making 42 fives altogether.

C)  Each of the digits 3 to 9 will have been used 42 times making a total of $42 \times 42 = 1764$. The number 1 has been used an extra 111 times making 153 and the number 2 an extra 24 times making $(42 + 24) \times 2$ i.e. 132. The grand total is then **2049**.

---

A new book was printed and the pages were numbered in the usual way. When these numbers were looked at it was noticed that a total of 555 digits had been used.

A)  How many pages were there in the book?

B)  How many fives were used?

C)  If all the digits used were added up, what would the total be?

---

*Solution No 2*

# Problem

## *Line Crossings*

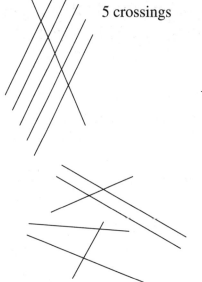

6 lines

5 crossings

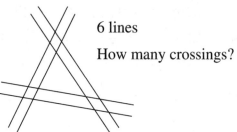

6 lines

How many crossings?

How many crossings

this time?

You will need to lengthen

some of the lines.

- Draw other arrangements of six lines.
- Count the number of crossings.
- What is the greatest number you can find?
- Can you be sure you have got them all?
- If there were *n* lines, what would the maximum number of crossings be?

*Problem No 3*

# Solution

## Line Crossings

Six lines lead to a maximum of 15 crossings.
In each case $n$ lines cross each of the other $(n-1)$ lines but each crossing has been counted twice leading to $\frac{1}{2}n(n-1)$ crossings in all i.e. the triangle numbers.
This *must* be all.

*Note: It is always possible to draw a line which is not parallel to any of the lines already drawn. Since non-parallel lines must always cross, the n th line crosses (n−1) others.*

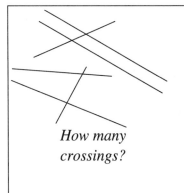

*How many crossings?*

- Draw other arrangements of six lines.
- Count the number of crossings.
- What is the greatest number you can find?
- Can you be sure you have got them all?
- If there were $n$ lines, what would the maximum number of crossings be?

*Solution No 3*

# Problem

## How Far?

Two men, starting at the same point, walk in opposite directions for four metres, then turn left and walk another three metres.
What is the distance between them?

*Problem No 4*

# Solution

## *How Far?*

10 metres.

They have each walked along two sides of a 3, 4, 5 right-angled triangle as shown:

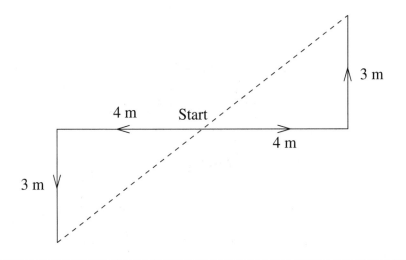

Two men, starting at the same point, walk in opposite directions for four metres, then turn left and walk another three metres.
What is the distance between them?

*Solution No 4*

# Problem

## *What time is it?*

Exactly how many minutes is it before six o'clock if, 50 minutes ago, it was four times as many minutes past three o'clock?

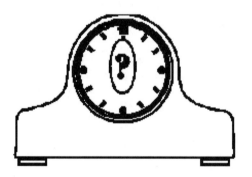

# Solution

*What time is it?*

It is **26** minutes to six.

Let $x$ be the number of minutes to six.

50 minutes ago the time was $x + 50$ minutes before six and also $4x$ minutes after three

$$\text{so } 4x + (x + 50) = 180. \text{ (Why?)}$$

Which solves to give $x = 26$.

---

Exactly how many minutes is it before six o'clock if, 50 minutes ago, it was four times as many minutes past three o'clock?

*Solution No 5*

# Problem

## *Fill it in*

Each of the letters A, B, C, D, E, and F has been written on a different face of a cube.

Four views of this cube are shown below.

Fill in the two missing letters on the last cube, remembering to make sure the letters are the correct way up.

# Solution

## *Fill it in*

Each of the letters A, B, C, D, E, and F has been written on a different face of a cube.

Four views of this cube are shown below.

Fill in the two missing letters on the last cube, remembering to make sure the letters are the correct way up.

# Problem

## *Matchsticks*

Given the following arrangement of twelve matchsticks:

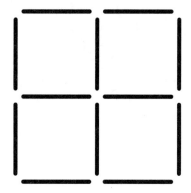

A)   Remove two matches to leave exactly two squares.

B)   Move three matches to leave exactly three squares.

## *Matchsticks*

A)

B)

Given the following arrangement of twelve matchsticks:

A)  Remove two matches to leave exactly two squares.

B)  Move three matches to leave exactly three squares.

# Problem

*Dominoes*

A set of dominoes contains tiles, each having two numbers between 0 and 6 (inclusive).

Each number is represented by a pattern of spots (0 is left blank).

Every possible pairing occurs just once, including each number with itself.

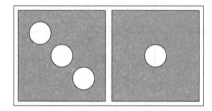

A)  How many dominoes are there in a set?

B)  What is the total number of spots in a set of dominoes?

# Solution

### *Dominoes*

A) There are 28 dominoes in a set.
   (Try listing them methodically and spot the pattern.)

B) Each of the numbers occurs eight times (twice on its double and then once with each of the other six numbers). This means that, since $8(0 + 1 + +2 + 3 + 4 + 5 + 6) = 168$, the total number of spots is 168.

---

A set of dominoes contains tiles, each having two numbers between 0 and 6 (inclusive).

Each number is represented by a pattern of spots (0 is left blank).

Every possible pairing occurs just once, including each number with itself.

A)   How many dominoes in a set?

B)   What is the total number of spots in a set of dominoes?

---

# Problem

## *Star Number*

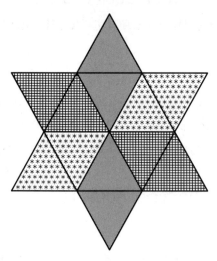

Fill in this star with the numbers 1, 2, …, 11, 12, one number to each triangle, so that the totals of the four numbers in the shaded diagonals (from point to opposite point) all give the same total.

# Solution

## *Star Number*

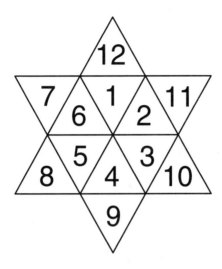

The total of the twelve numbers 1, 2, …, 11, 12 is 78. Since there are three diagonals, the numbers of each one must add up to 78 ÷ 3 = 26. In the solution above, each half diagonal totals 13 but the order on a diagonal is unimportant.

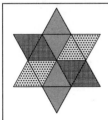
Fill in this star with the numbers 1, 2, …, 11, 12, one number to each triangle, so that the totals of the four numbers in the shaded diagonals (from point to opposite point) all give the same total.

*Solution No 9*

# Problem

## *Triangles*

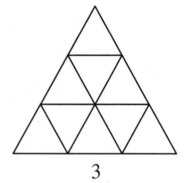

| 1 | 2 | 3 |

A)   How many small triangles are there in each of the diagrams shown above?

B)   How many in each of the next two?
(Either draw them or explain your answer.)

C)   *Without drawing*, how many would there be in the 25th diagram?

D)   Can a diagram in the series have
(i) 961 triangles or (ii) 1000 triangles?   (Explain your answer.)

# Solution

### *Triangles*

A)  1, 4, 9.

B)  16, 25 because each triangle is split into $n^2$ small ones.  (Can you see why?)

C)  $25^2 = 625$ triangles.

D)  961 *is* possible because it is the square of 31  but 1000 is not a perfect square and so does not fit the pattern.

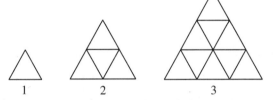

A)  How many small triangles are there in each of the diagrams shown above?

B)  How many in each of the next two?
    (Either draw them or explain your answer.)

C)  *Without drawing*, how many would there be in the 25th diagram?

D)  Can a diagram in the series have  (i) 961 triangles,
    or (ii) 1000 triangles?
    (Explain your answer).

*Solution No 10*

# Problem

### *Shady Question*

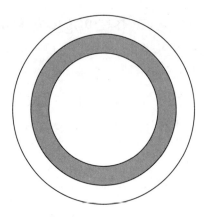

The three circles in the diagram have the same centre and have radii 3cm, 4cm and 5cm.

What percentage of the largest circle is shaded?

# Solution

## Shady Question

Remembering that the area of a circle is $\pi r^2$, the shaded area is $\pi \left(4^2 - 3^2\right)$.

So the fraction is $\dfrac{\pi \left(4^2 - 3^2\right)}{\pi\,5^2}$.

Which comes to $\dfrac{7}{25}$ or 28%

The three circles in the diagram have the same centre and have radii 3cm, 4cm and 5cm.
What percentage of the largest circle is shaded?

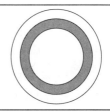

*Solution No 11*

# Problem

## *Train Set*

Jonathan has two circular railway lines, one with an inner diameter of 3 metres and the other with an inner diameter of 4 metres.

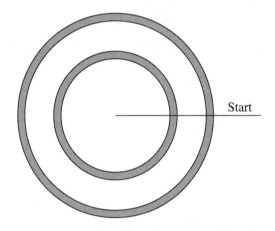

Start

He runs an engine clockwise round each track at the same speed, starting at the same time from the start line shown in the diagram.

What are the relative positions of the trains when the train on the shorter track has made 11 complete circuits?

*Problem No 12*

# Solution

## *Train Set*

On the shorter track, 11 circuits come to a total of $33\pi$ metres.

One circuit of the longer track is $4\pi$ metres, so the engine travels $\dfrac{33\pi}{4\pi} = 8\frac{1}{4}$ times round and is at the point $P$ on the circle.

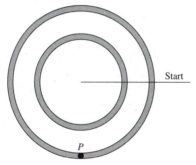

Jonathan has two circular railway lines, one with an inner diameter of 3 metres and the other with an inner diameter of 4 metres.

He runs an engine clockwise round each track at the same speed, starting at the same time from the start line shown in the diagram.

What are the relative positions of the trains when the train on the shorter track has made 11 complete circuits?

*Solution No 12*

# Problem

### Symbols

Each symbol stands for a different number.

The totals of five of the rows or columns are shown.

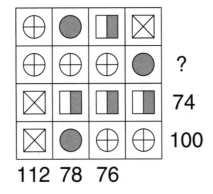

A) What number does each symbol stand for?

B) What is the total shown by '?'

## *Symbols*

⬤ = 20          ⊠ = 32

⊕ = 24          ▯ = 14

Use the second and third columns to find the value of
⬤ and then the bottom row and first column to work
out ⊠ and ⊕, ▯ then follows.

This gives the value of '?' as 92.

Each symbol stands for a
different number.
The totals of five of the rows or
columns are shown.

A)  What number does each symbol
    stand for?

B)  What is the total shown by '?'

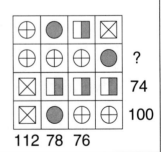

*Solution No 13*

# Problem

### *Square Pieces*

The diagram shows a square, divided by three equally spaced horizontal lines and the left to right diagonal.
Between the lines, there is shading, starting at the top left, then alternately to the right and left.

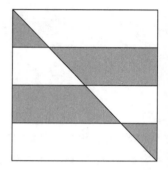

A) What fraction of the square is shaded?

B) If there was only one horizontal line, what fraction would be shaded?

C) What about two horizontal lines ? or four?

D) Can you find a general rule $n$ lines?

# Solution

## *Square Pieces*

This question becomes easier to answer if the square is split into small squares by putting in vertical lines.

A)  3/8          B)  1/4          C)  both 1/2

D)  An *even* number of lines always leads to the fraction shaded being half.

An odd number of lines leads to the sequence of fractions 1/4,  3/8,  5/12,  7/16, ….

For *n* lines, when *n* is odd, the fraction shaded is

then $\dfrac{n}{2(n+1)}$. (Can you explain why?)

---

The diagram shows a square, divided by three equally spaced horizontal lines and the left to right diagonal.

Between the lines, there is shading, starting at the top left, then alternately to the right and left.

A)  What fraction of the square is shaded?

B)  If there was only one horizontal line, what fraction would be shaded?

C)  What about two horizontal lines ? or four?

D)  Can you find a general rule *n* lines?

---

*Solution No 14*

# Problem

## *The Hungry Woodworm*

A hungry woodworm finds a cubical block made of 27 small cubes, each of a different kind of wood. "What a feast!" the woodworm thinks, "I should like to taste all these woods, finishing up in the middle one for a sleep."

The woodworm must
(i)   start from outside the block,
(ii)  enter and leave each cube by the centre of one of its faces,
(iii) pass through each small cube just once,
(iv)  end up in the cube in the middle of the block.

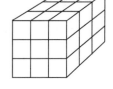

Can the woodworm enjoy his 27-course meal and end up in the centre for his rest?

If so, how?

If not, why not?

## *The Hungry Woodworm*

To finish in the centre cube, the worm must eat
through the 26 cubes with external faces.
Imagine the cubes shaded as shown. To satisfy
the rules, the worm must follow a path which
alternates from a black cube **b** to a white cube **w**
taking in all 26 outer cubes and then enter the
centre cube (which is white). But there are 14 black cubes and 13 white
cubes and the required *alternating* sequence must end with a white cube
which is impossible.

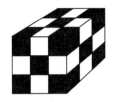

A hungry woodworm finds a cubical
block made of 27 small cubes, each of
different kinds of wood.
"What a feast!" the woodworm thinks,
"I should like to taste all these woods,
finishing up in the middle one for a
sleep." The woodworm must
(i)    start from outside the block,
(ii)   enter and leave each cube by the centre of one of its faces,
(iii)  pass through each small cube just once,
(iv)  end up in the cube in the middle of the block.

Can the woodworm enjoy his 27-course meal and end up in the
centre for his rest? If so, how? If not, why not?

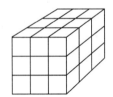

# Problem

## *Grid Puzzle*

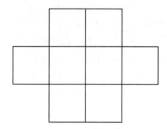

Arrange the numbers 1, 2, 3, 4, 5, 6, 7 and 8 in the blank grid in such a way that no two consecutive numbers must be in boxes that touch either along an edge or at a corner.

*The grid shown here is **not** a solution because 6 and 7 and 1 and 2 touch at a corner and 5 and 6 along an edge.*

|   | 1 | 4 |   |
|---|---|---|---|
| 3 | 7 | 2 | 8 |
|   | 5 | 6 |   |

*Problem No 16*

## *Grid Puzzle*

A solution is:

|   | 4 | 6 |   |
|---|---|---|---|
| 7 | 1 | 8 | 2 |
|   | 3 | 5 |   |

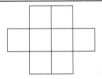

Arrange the numbers 1, 2, 3, 4, 5, 6, 7 and 8 in the blank grid in the such a way that no two consecutive numbers must be in boxes that touch either along an edge or at a corner.

*(The grid shown here is **not** a solution because 6 and 7 and 1 and 2 touch at a corner and 5 and 6 along an edge.)*

|   | 1 | 4 |   |
|---|---|---|---|
| 3 | 7 | 2 | 8 |
|   | 5 | 6 |   |

*Solution No 16*

# Problem

## *Some Sums*

In each of the following sums, each letter stands for a different number. See if you can work out what each should say.

(There may be more than one answer in some cases.)

① 
$$
\begin{array}{r}
FOUR \\
+ ONE \\
\hline
FIVE
\end{array}
$$

And in French!

② 
$$
\begin{array}{r}
MOI \\
+ TOI \\
\hline
NOUS
\end{array}
$$

Try division:

③ 
$$
A \overline{)HAPPY}^{\,XMAS}
$$

*Problem No 17*

# Solution

## *Some Sums*

Possible solutions are:

1.
$$
\begin{array}{r}
1470 \\
+\ 458 \\
\hline
1928
\end{array}
$$

And, in French:

2.
$$
\begin{array}{r}
523 \\
+\ 723 \\
\hline
1246
\end{array}
$$

Division:

3.
$$
7\overline{)67004} = 9572
$$

---

① FOUR
+ ONE
FIVE

② **MOI**
**+ TOI**
**NOUS**

③ **XMAS**
**A ⌐HAPPY**

In each of the following sums, each letter stands for a different number. See if you can work out what each should say. (There may be more than one answer in each case.)

---

# Problem

## *What Number?*

What is the four digit number, with no zeros, in which the first digit is five times the last, the second is four more than the first and three times the third, and the third is two more than the last and two less than the first?

*Problem No 18*

# Solution

## *What Number?*

The number is **5931.**

No zeros are allowed so, because the first figure is five times the last figure they must be 5 and 1 respectively. The rest follows directly.

---

What is the four digit number, with no zeros, in which the first digit is five times the last, the second is four more than the first and three times the third, and the third is two more than the last and two less than the first?

---

*Solution No 18*

# Problem

## *Typists*

If two typists can type two pages in two minutes, how many typists will it take to type eighteen pages in six minutes?

# Solution

## *Typists*

Each typist takes two minutes to type a page so can type three pages in six minutes. This means that 6 typists will be needed for 18 pages.

If two typists can type two pages in two minutes, how many typists will it take to type eighteen pages in six minutes?

# Problem

## *Angle Size*

In the diagram shown (which is *not* drawn accurately), two lines meet at *O* making an angle of $x°$.

*A*, *B* and *C* are constructed so that *OA* = *OB* = *OC*.

Find *y* in terms of *x*.

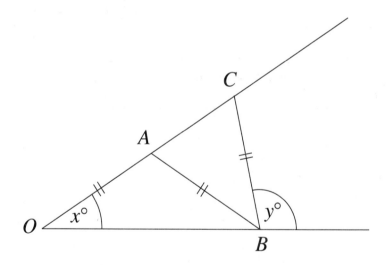

*Problem No 20*

# Solution

## *Angle Size*

$y = 3x$

By looking at the angles of $\triangle OAB$, or at the exterior angle of a triangle, it can be seen that
$\angle BAC = \angle BCA = 2x°$
(exterior angle of a triangle = the sum of opposite interior angles).

Now $\qquad \angle ABC = (180 - 4x)°$

and $\qquad \angle OBA = x°.$

So $\quad y = 180 - x - (180 - 4x)$

$\qquad = 3x$ (or use the exterior angle of $\triangle OBC$).

In the diagram shown (which is *not* drawn accurately), two lines meet at $O$ making an angle of $x°$.
$A$, $B$ and $C$ are constructed so that $OA = OB = OC$.
Find $y$ in terms of $x$.

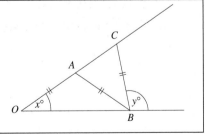

*Solution No 20*

# Problem

## *Grey Areas*

In the two squares shown below, the midpoints of each side have been marked and then joined to the vertices in different ways. The rhombus in the centre has been shaded each time.

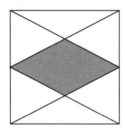 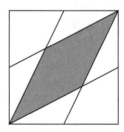

A)  What fraction of the square is shaded in each case?

B)  What happens if the square becomes a rhombus or a rectangle or a parallelogram?
    Is the fraction the same?

# Solution

## Grey Areas

A) In the first case **1/4** of the square is shaded.

*(To convince yourself, join the horizontal diagonal of the shaded rhombus, and look at the areas of the triangles formed.)*

In the second case **1/3** is shaded.

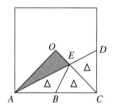

This diagram shows some parts of the second diagram. Triangles *OAC* and *ACD* are each a quarter of the square. △*ACD* is divided into thirds by the lines *EB* and *EC*. (△s *ABE* and *EBC* have equal bases and the same height. △s *EBC* and *EDC* are congruent.) So each of △s *ABE*, *EBC* and *EDC* has an area, △, which is one third of a quarter of the area of the square. So area of the shaded triangle is also △. Hence the rhombus is 4/12 = 1/3 of the area of the square.

B) The same results hold for these shapes.

In the two squares shown, the midpoints of each side have been marked and then joined to the vertices in different ways. The rhombus in the centre has been shaded each time.

A) What fraction of the square is shaded in each case?

B) What happens if the square becomes a rhombus, a rectangle or a parallelogram? Is the fraction the same?

*Solution No 21*

# Problem

## *Can You Solve It?*

$$a + b + c + d = 20$$
$$a - b + c + d = 10$$
$$a + b - c + d = 14$$
$$a + b + c - d = 16$$

Find the values of $a$, $b$, $c$ and $d$.

# Solution

*Can You Solve It?*

A possible method:

$$a + b + c + d = 20 \qquad (1)$$
$$a - b + c + d = 10 \qquad (2)$$
$$a + b - c + d = 14 \qquad (3)$$
$$a + b + c - d = 16 \qquad (4)$$

(1) − (2)   gives   $2b = 10$   so   $b = 5.$
(1) − (3)   gives   $2c = 6$   so   $c = 3.$
(1) − (4)   gives   $2d = 4$   so   $d = 2.$

The values of $b$, $c$ and $d$ lead to the value of $a$.

**$a = 10, b = 5, c = 3$ and $d = 2.$**

$$a + b + c + d = 20$$
$$a - b + c + d = 10$$
$$a + b - c + d = 14$$
$$a + b + c - d = 16$$

Find the values of $a$, $b$, $c$ and $d$.

*Solution No 22*

# Problem

## Square Root

What is the square root of
123456789987654321?

(Try to work it out without using a computer.)

*(Hint: Look at the patterns formed by $11^2$, $111^2$ etc)*

*Problem No 23*

# Solution

## *Square Root*

If you think about the structure of a long multiplication you can see what is happening:

```
        1 1 1                           1 1 1 1
      × 1 1 1                       ×   1 1 1 1
      -------                       -----------
        1 1 1                           1 1 1 1
      1 1 1 0                         1 1 1 1 0
    1 1 1 0 0                       1 1 1 1 0 0
    ---------                     1 1 1 1 0 0 0
    1 2 3 2 1                     ---------------
                                   1 2 3 4 3 2 1
```

So the answer is

$$\sqrt{12345678987654321} = 111111111.$$

---

 What is the square root of
12345678987654321?
(Try without a computer!)

---

*Solution No 23*

# Problem

## *Find The Difference*

Squares with edges of 2 centimetres and 3 centimetres overlap as shown.

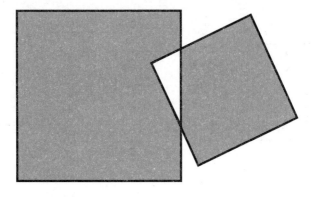

What is the difference between the areas of the two shaded parts?

*Problem No 24*

## *Find the Difference*

The difference is **5 cm²**.

If the white area is $A$ cm², the larger shaded part is $(9 - A)$ cm² and the smaller is $(4 - A)$ cm² , and

$$(9 - A) - (4 - A) = 9 - A - 4 + A = 5.$$

So the difference between the areas is always the same, however they overlap.

Squares with edges of 2 centimetres and 3 centimetres overlap as shown.

What is the difference between the areas of the two shaded parts?

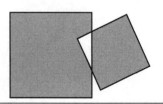

*Solution No 24*

# Problem

*Cows*

A farmer has 41 cows and lives in a house surrounded by 8 fields.

There is a window in each side of the house and he can see three of the fields from each of the windows.

How should the cows be put into the fields so that exactly 15 cows can be seen from each of the windows?

# Solution

## *Cows*

A possible solution is:

| | | |
|:---:|:---:|:---:|
| 5 | 6 | 4 |
| 6 | **House** | 5 |
| 4 | 5 | 6 |

A farmer has 41 cows and lives in a house surrounded by 8 fields.

There is a window in each side of the house and he can see three of the fields from each of the windows.

How should the cows be placed in the fields so that exactly 15 cows can be seen from each of the windows?

# Problem

*Prove It*

A circle touches two perpendicular lines, which cross at *O*, at *C* and *D*.  *A* and *B* lie on *OC* and *OD* such that *AB* is a tangent to the circle, touching it at *X*.

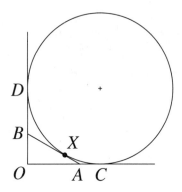

Show that the perimeter of the triangle *AOB* is equal to the diameter of the circle.

# Solution

## *Prove It*

Let the radius of the circle be $r$.

$$OD = OC = r.$$

(They form a square with the centre of the circle.)

$$AX = AC$$

(Tangents from a point are equal.)

So $\quad OA + OX = OA + AC = r.$

Similarly $\quad OB + BX = r.$

Thus $\quad OA + AX + XB + OB = 2r.$

But $OA + AX + XB + OB$ form the perimeter of the triangle $OAB$.

So the perimeter of the triangle is equal to the diameter of the circle.

---

A circle touches two perpendicular lines, which cross at $O$, at $C$ and $D$. $A$ and $B$ lie on $OC$ and $OD$ such that $AB$ is a tangent to the circle, touching it at $X$.

Show that the perimeter of the triangle $AOB$ is equal to the diameter of the circle.

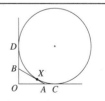

---

*Solution No 26*

# Problem

*Adding It Up*

```
      THREE
      THREE
  +    FOUR
  ─────────
     ELEVEN
```

If each letter stands for a different digit, what is the value of each one?

# Solution

## *Adding It Up*

A possible solution is:

$$
\begin{array}{r}
78011 \\
78011 \\
+\ 5390 \\
\hline
161412
\end{array}
$$

| If each letter stands for a different digit, what is the value of each one? | THREE |
|---|---|
| | THREE |
| | +  FOUR |
| | ELEVEN |

*Solution No 27*

# Problem

## *Fun with Factorials*

The factorial of a number (shown by '!') means that the number is multiplied by all the numbers smaller than itself, counting down to one.  For example
$4! = 4 \times 3 \times 2 \times 1 = 24$.

Check that you agree that $5! = 120$

Work out 10!
(You should find that it ends with two zeros.)

Without working out the value, how many zeros will there be at the end of 100!

# Solution

## *Fun with Factorials*

There are **24** zeros.

Zeros only occur when the previous product is multiplied by a number ending in 5 or in 0 (can you explain why?), i.e. any multiples of 5. There are 19 multiples of 5 less than 100 so there are 19 + 3 fives in 100! (+ 3 because 25, 50, 75 each have 2 fives as factors) leading to 22 zeros and then the number is multiplied by 100 adding two more.

---

The factorial of a number (shown by '!') means that the number is multiplied by all the numbers smaller than itself, counting down to one. For example 4! = 4 × 3 × 2 × 1 = 24.

Check that you agree that 5! = 120

Work out 10!
(You should find that it ends with two zeros.)

Without working out the value, how many zeros will there be at the end of 100!

---

# Problem

## *How Big?*

What is the area of a triangle with sides 13 cm, 14 cm and 15 cm?

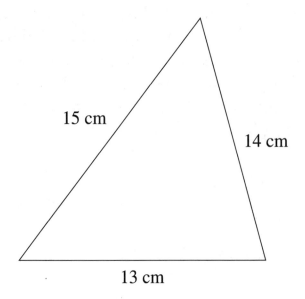

# Solution

## *How Big?*

The area is **84 cm²**.

This can be worked out using by Pythagoras' theorem to find the height of the triangle but it involves some algebra or using the sine and cosine rules to find an angle and then the height (or the formula that the area of a triangle is $\frac{1}{2}ab$ sin $C$).

There is also a formula (known as Heron's formula) which states that $A = \sqrt{s(s-a)(s-b)(s-c)}$, where $s$ is half the perimeter of the triangle, in this case 21cm, and $a$, $b$, $c$ are the lengths of the sides. The area is then $\sqrt{21 \times 6 \times 7 \times 8} = 84$.

What is the area of a triangle with sides 13 cm, 14 cm and 15 cm?

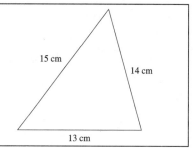

*Solution No 29*

# Problem

## *A Magic Hexagon*

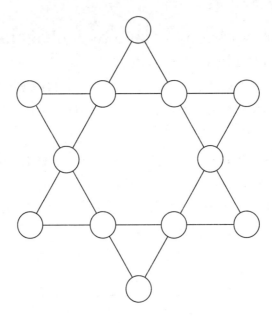

Try to place all of the numbers 1 to 12 in the circles so that the four numbers in each line add up to 26.

*Problem No 30*

# Solution

## *A Magic Hexagon*

A possible solution is:

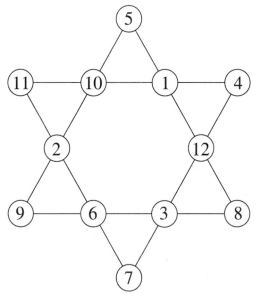

Try to place all of the numbers 1 to
12 in the circles so that the four
numbers in each line add up to 26.

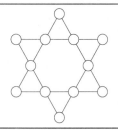

*Solution No 30*

# Problem

## *Why does it happen?*

Take any five consecutive numbers, for example 5, 6, 7, 8 and 9.

Ignore the middle number and multiply the first with the last and the second with the fourth (as shown below).

Then take the difference of these two products.

$$5 \ 6 \ 7 \ 8 \ 9$$

$$48 - 45 = 3.$$

Try with another set of five consecutive numbers. The answer should be 3 again.

Explain why the answer is always 3.

*Problem No 31*

# Solution

### *Why does it happen?*

It is best to use algebra to show this.
Let the middle number be $n$,
then the numbers are

$$n - 2, n - 1, n, n + 1, n + 2.$$

Multiplying gives

$$(n - 1)(n + 1) = n^2 - 1$$

and

$$(n - 2)(n + 2) = n^2 - 4.$$

Subtracting: $(n^2 - 1) - (n^2 - 4) = 3.$

---

Take any five consecutive numbers, for
example 5, 6, 7, 8 and 9.

Ignore the middle number and multiply
the first with the last and the second with
the fourth (as shown).

Then take the difference of these two products.

$$48 - 45 = 3.$$

Try with another set of five consecutive numbers. The answer
should be 3 again.

Explain why the answer is always 3.

---

*Solution No 31*

# Problem

## *Eighty One*

A)  The sum of three consecutive numbers is 81.
    What are the numbers?

B)  Can you find three consecutive numbers which
    add up to 100?

# Solution

### *Eighty One*

A)  The numbers are **26, 27 and 28**.
    The sum of three consecutive numbers is three
    times the middle one. (*See if you can show this
    using algebra.*)
    This means that the middle number can be found
    by simply dividing 81 by 3.

B)  This is not possible because 100 does not divide
    exactly by three.

---

(???)

A) The sum of three consecutive numbers is 81. What are the
   numbers?
B) Can you find three consecutive numbers which add up to
   100?

!!!

---

*Solution No 32*

# Problem

## *Noughts and Crosses*

In a game of noughts and crosses, the first player to get 3 in a line is the winner.

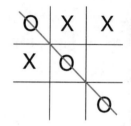

There are 8 possible winning lines, 3 rows, 3 columns and 2 diagonals.

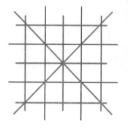

3-dimensional noughts and crosses has three layers of 3 by 3.

How many winning lines are there now?

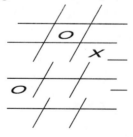

# Solution

## *Noughts and Crosses*

There are now 49 winning lines.

3 sets of 8 as before, 9 vertical lines, 12 diagonals in vertical planes, and 4 full diagonals. (A full diagonal goes from a corner in the top layer, through the centre of the middle layer and comes out at the opposite corner on the bottom layer,)

In a game of noughts and crosses, the first player to get 3 in a line is the winner.
There are 8 possible winning lines, 3 rows, 3 columns and 2 diagonals.
3-dimensional noughts and crosses has three layers of 3 by 3. How many winning lines are there now?

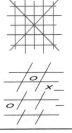

*Solution No 33*

# Problem

## *Chess Board Problem*

If the only moves allowed are one square to the right or one square down, it takes fourteen moves to get from the top left hand corner to the bottom right.

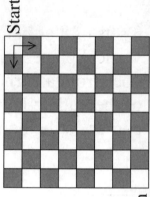

How many *different* 14 move routes are there from the top left to the bottom right?

# Solution

## *Chess Board Problem*

There are **3432** ways.

Taking a 2 by 2 square and then a 3 by 3 square etc, the number of routes goes 2, 6, 20, 70, ….

For an $n$ by $n$ board, each route will have length $2n - 2$ squares (why?). To get from the top left corner to the bottom right corner, $n - 1$ right turns must be made (why?). So the number of routes is the number of ways to choose $n - 1$ turns from $2n - 2$ steps. This is $\dfrac{(2n - 2)!}{(n - 1)! \times (n - 1)!}$ or $^{2n-2}C_{n-1}$.

---

If the only moves allowed are one square to the right or one square down, it takes fourteen moves to get from the top left hand corner to the bottom right.

How many **different** 14 move routes are there from the top left to the bottom right?

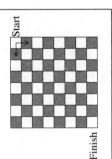

---

*Solution No 34*

*Feed the Fly!*

A cylindrical glass is 8 cm high and 12 cm in circumference.

On the *inside*, 2 cm from the top, is a drop of honey.

On the *outside*, 2 cm from the bottom, on the opposite side of the glass, is a fly.

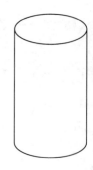

What is the shortest route from the fly to the honey?

# Solution

## *Feed the Fly!*

The shortest route covers **10 cm**.

*Imagine cutting the curved surface of the glass and laying it flat so that it forms a rectangle. The fly is 2 cm from the bottom of the rectangle and the honey 2 cm from the top on the opposite side and the horizontal separation is 6 cm, half the circumference.*

*The shortest route is for the fly to aim towards a point 2 cm **above** this rectangle, a reflection of the position of the honey in the rim of the glass.*

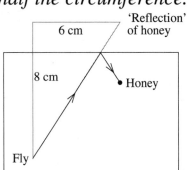

A cylindrical glass is 8 cm high and 12 cm in circumference.

On the inside, 2 cm from the top, is a drop of honey.

On the outside, 2 cm from the bottom, on the opposite side of the glass, is a fly.

What is the shortest route from the fly to the honey?

*Solution No 35*

# Problem

*Make a Million!*

Find two numbers,
neither of which has a zero digit,
whose product is
1 000 000.

*Problem No 36*

# Solution

## *Make a Million!*

The numbers are **64** and **15625.**

If you split 1 000 000 into prime factors, you get $2^6 \times 5^6$. Any time a 5 is multiplied by a 2 a zero results so the factors must be $2^6$ and $5^6$.

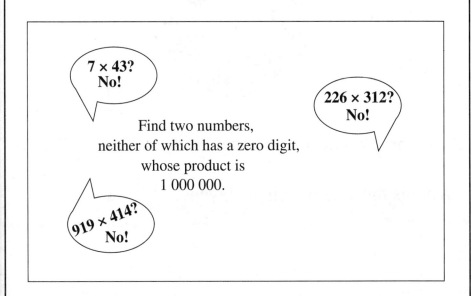

*Solution No 36*

# Problem

## *CD Space*

The playing area of a CD is the outer ring (shown shaded in the diagram below).

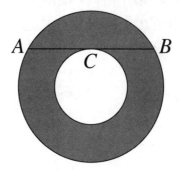

The line *AB* touches the inner circle at *C* and is 10 cm long.

What is the area which is played?

*Problem No 37*

# Solution

## *CD Space*

The area is **$25\pi$ cm²**.

Suppose the radius of the larger circle is $R$ and of the smaller circle is $r$. Then the shaded area is

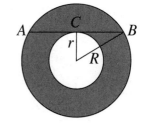

$$\pi R^2 - \pi r^2 = \pi\left(R^2 - r^2\right).$$

But, using Pythagoras,

$$R^2 - r^2 = CB^2$$

$$= 5^2$$

$$= 25.$$

---

The playing area of a CD is the outer ring (shown shaded in the diagram).

The line $AB$ touches the inner circle at $C$ and is 10 cm long.

What is the area which is played?

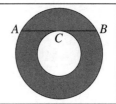

---

*Solution No 37*

# Problem

## *Pentagon Pieces*

A pentagon is formed by constructing a right-angled isosceles triangle on the top of a square with edges 2 cm long as shown.

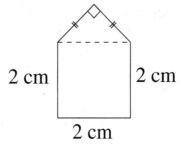

2 cm

2 cm

2 cm

A) What is the area of the pentagon?

B) How can the pentagon be cut into three pieces which can be put together to form another square?

*Problem No 38*

# Solution

### *Pentagon Pieces*

A)    The area is **5 cm²**.

Imagine reflecting the isosceles triangle in the dotted line. So you can see that the area of the triangle is $\frac{1}{4}$ of the area of the square and so it is 1 cm².

B)    Joining the midpoint of a side of the square to a vertex gives a length of √5 (can you see why?) so this gives us the length of a side of the new square.
Can you see how the pieces fit together to make a square?

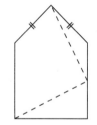

---

A pentagon is formed by constructing a right-angled isosceles triangle on the top of a square with 2 cm edges as shown.

A)    What is the area of the pentagon?

B)    How can the pentagon be cut into three pieces which can be put together to form another square?

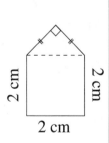

2 cm

2 cm

2 cm

---

*Solution No 38*

# Problem

## *A Question of Algebra*

Work out the values of the whole numbers $a$ and $b$ in the following simultaneous equations:

$$a + b = 8$$

$$\frac{1}{a} + \frac{1}{b} = \frac{2}{3}$$

# Solution

## *A Question of Algebra*

$a = 2$ and $b = 6$ (or the other way round).

(Though this can be solved algebraically, it can also be worked out by finding pairs of numbers to fit the first equation and trying to fit them into the second.)

Work out the values of the whole numbers $a$ and $b$ in the following simultaneous equations:

$$a + b = 8$$

$$\frac{1}{a} + \frac{1}{b} = \frac{2}{3}$$

*Solution No 39*

# Problem

## *School Run*

There are three different paths John can use to get to school. When he gets there, he can use any of three gates into the playground and even a hole in the fence he has found! There are two doors into the building itself.

John decides to use a different route every day for as long as he can. How many days can he keep doing this?

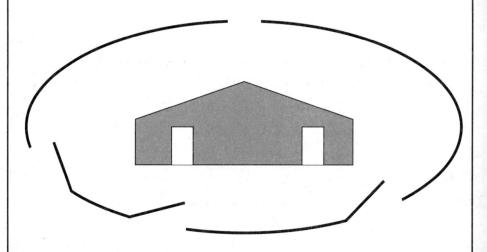

*Problem No 40*

# Solution

## *School Run*

He can do this in **24** different ways so he will take **24** days over it.

(Each of the three routes can be combined with each of the four ways into the playground and these twelve different routes to school can each be combined with either of the two doors.)

There are three different paths John can use to get to school. When he gets there, he can use any of three gates into the playground and even a hole in the fence he has found! There are two doors into the building itself.

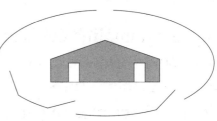

John decides to use a different route every day for as long as he can. How many days can he keep doing this?

# **Problem**

## *An angular question*

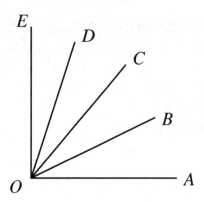

In the diagram, line *OA* is at right angles to line *OE*.
How many different angles, not greater than 90°, are
there altogether? (There are more than 4.)

With five lines meeting at a point, similar to those
shown, how would you place them to get the smallest
number of different sizes of angle?

What about the largest number of different sizes?

*Problem No 41*

# Solution

### *An angular question*

There are **10** angles altogether.

(If you are not sure about this try listing them using the three letters e.g. *AOC*, remembering that every angle must include the letter *O*.)

If each of the small acute angles is 22½° then there are just four different sizes.

If all the small angles are *different* in such a way that no combinations add to the same, you should get all ten angles different. e.g. 2°, 17°, 32° and 39° (There are many ways to do this.)

---

In the diagram, line *OA* is at right angles to line *OE*. How many different angles, not greater than 90°, are there altogether? (There are more than 4.)

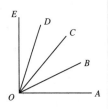

With five lines meeting at a point, similar to those shown, how would you place them to get the smallest number of different sizes of angle?

What about the largest number of different sizes?

---

*Solution No 41*

# Problem

## *Ring the changes*

If you are interested in campanology (bell-ringing) you will see that there is a lot of mathematics involved. Bells A, B, C and D can be rung in any order except that, only two adjacent bells can change places, so A, B, C, D can be followed by B, A, D, C but **not** by A, D, C, B.

(You need to remember that the four bells are rung again and again e.g. A,B,C,D, A,B,C,D, …. so A and D can change.)

Work out how all of the 24 possible arrangements of the bells can be rung, starting and ending with A, B, C, D.

# Solution

## *Ring the changes*

A possible solution is:

| | | | |
|---|---|---|---|
| A,B,C,D | B,C,A,D | C,D,B,A | D,A,C,B |
| B,A,C,D | C,B,D,A | D,C,A,B | A,D,B,C |
| B,A,D,C | C,B,A,D | D,C,B,A | A,D,C,B |
| B,D,A,C | C,A,B,D | D,B,C,A | A,C,D,B |
| B,D,C,A | C,A,D,B | D,B,A,C | A,C,B,D |
| B,C,D,A | C,D,A,B | D,A,B,C | A,B,D,C |
| | | | A,B,C,D |

If you are interested in campanology (bell ringing) you will see that there is a lot of Mathematics involved. Bells A, B, C and D can be rung in any order except that, only two adjacent bells can change places, so A,B,C,D can be followed by B,A,D,C but not by A,D,C,B.

(You need to remember that the four bells are rung again and again e.g. A,B,C,D,A,B,C,D,…. so A and D can change.)

Work out how all of the 24 possible arrangements of the bells can be rung, starting and ending with A,B,C,D.

*Solution No 42*

# Problem

## *An age old question*

Tom and his sister Jenny were born on the same date but in different years.

Tom has noticed that, two years ago, he was three times as old as Jenny but that, in two years time, he will only be twice her age.

How old are they now?

When was Jenny a fifth of Tom's age?

# Solution

### *An age old question*

Let Tom's age now be $t$ and Jenny's be $j$.
Two years ago

$$t - 2 = 3(j - 2) = 3j - 6$$

and in two year's time

$$t + 2 = 2(j + 2) = 2j + 4.$$

Solving these simultaneously gives $t = 14$ and
$j = 6$ so

**Tom is 14 and Jenny is 6.**

When Tom was 10, Jenny was only 2, one fifth of his
age, i.e. 4 years ago.

---

Tom and his sister Jenny were born on the same date but in different years.

Tom has noticed that, two years ago, he was three times as old as Jenny but that, in two years time, he will only be twice her age.

How old are they now?

When was Jenny a fifth of Tom's age?

---

*Solution No 43*

# Problem

## *Bags of shopping*

Mrs Kahn has three different bags she can take to the shops with her.

The first can take two bags of sugar and three cans or four bags of sugar and one can.

The second can take one bottle of milk and two bags of sugar or one can and three bottles of milk.

The third will hold three bottles of milk and three cans.

If she puts just one bottle of milk into the third bag, how many bags of sugar will fit in?

*Problem No 44*

# Solution

## *Bags of shopping*

She can fit in 4 bags of sugar.

*(Use algebra to work out the following:*
If you look at the first bag, you should be able to work out that a bag of sugar is actually equivalent to a can.
The second bag should lead you to realise that two bottles of milk are equivalent to one can or bag of sugar so the space taken up by two bottles in the third can be replaced by one bag of sugar and the three cans can be replaced by three bags of sugar making four in all.)

---

Mrs Kahn has three different bags she can take to the shops with her.
The first can take two bags of sugar and three cans or four bags of sugar and one can.
The second can take one bottle of milk and two bags of sugar or one can and three bottles of milk.
The third will hold three bottles of milk and three cans. If she puts just one bottle of milk into the third bag, how many bags of sugar will fit in?

---

*Solution No 44*

# Problem

## *Winner takes all*

Two friends decide to play a game with ten cards, numbered from 1 to 10, placed face up on the table. They take it in turns to choose a card following these rules:

- The first player can choose any card but, from that point onwards, the card chosen must have a number which is either a factor or a multiple of the previous one.
- The first player who cannot go, loses the game.

Which player should be able to win and how?

# Solution

## *Winner takes all*

The **second** player, B, can always win the game.

In most cases, B forces a strategy which involves the first, A, eventually having to play the card numbered 1 and then this is followed by B playing 7 leaving no moves for A.

So, if A starts with a 1, B plays 7, A playing 2 needs B to play 6, 3 needs 9, 4 needs 8, 5 needs 10, 6 needs 2, 8 needs 4, 9 needs 3 and 10 needs 5. If A starts with 7 B has to play 1 and then A has a free choice but B still wins using the next move listed above.

Two friends decide to play a game with ten cards, numbered from 1 to 10, placed face up on the table.

They take it in turns to choose a card following these rules:

- The first player can choose any card but, from that point onwards, the card chosen must have a number which is either a factor or a multiple of the previous one.
- The first player who cannot go, loses the game.

Which player should be able to win and how?

*Solution No 45*

# Problem

## *Bisection*

David was in a maths exam and had been asked to find the perpendicular bisector of a line 12 centimetres long using pencil, ruler and compasses only.  To his horror, when he got out his compasses, he discovered that they had been broken by his little sister and would only draw circles of radius 2.5 centimetres.

How did he manage to get full marks on this question?

## *Bisection*

Using his compasses David could mark off points 2.5 cm from each end of the line and then, using his compasses again, could mark off points 5 cm from each end and finally could find the perpendicular bisector of the resulting 2 cm portion in the normal way.

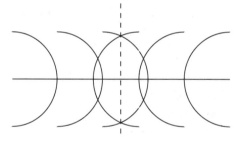

David was in a maths exam and had been asked to bisect a line 12 centimetres long using pencil, ruler and compasses only. To his horror, when he got out his compasses, he discovered that they had been broken by his little sister and would only draw circles of radius 2.5 centimetres. How did he manage to get full marks on this question?

# Problem

## *How likely?*

A game is played on triangular grid as shown.  On the throw of a die, a counter is moved from one dot to an adjacent one, the number on the die showing what direction to move in (as shown).

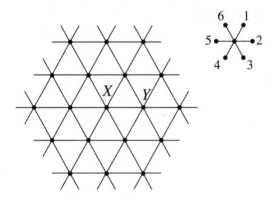

A counter starts at point *X*.  What is the probability that after two moves it will be at point *Y*?

*Problem No 47*

# Solution

## *How likely?*

The only ways to get from *X* to *Y* in two moves are by throwing a 1 followed by a 3 or a 3 followed by a 1.

Each if these can be done with probability $\frac{1}{36}$ so the final probability is $\frac{2}{36}$ or $\frac{1}{18}$.

A game is played on triangular grid as shown. On the throw of a dice a counter is moved from one dot to an adjacent one, the number on the dice showing what direction to move in (as shown).

A counter starts at point *X*. What is the probability that after two moves it will be at point *Y*?

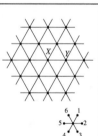

# Problem

### *Late again!*

A commuter has been checking on how many minutes late her train is each evening over the last few weeks and has come up with the following results:

| Number of minutes late ($m$) | Number of times |
|:---:|:---:|
| $m \leqslant 1$ | 0 |
| $1 < m \leqslant 2$ | 5 |
| $2 < m \leqslant 3$ | 12 |
| $3 < m \leqslant 4$ | 3 |
| $4 < m \leqslant 5$ | 2 |
| $5 < m$ | 3 |

Based on these results, estimate the probability that her train is more than three minutes late.

*Problem No 48*

# Solution

## *Late again!*

Eight of the twenty-five trains are more than three minutes late so the probability is $\dfrac{8}{25} = 0{\cdot}32$.

A commuter has been checking on how many minutes late her train is each evening over the last few weeks and has come up with the following results:

| Number of minutes late ($m$) | Number of times |
|---|---|
| $m \leqslant 1$ | 0 |
| $1 < m \leqslant 2$ | 5 |
| $2 < m \leqslant 3$ | 12 |
| $3 < m \leqslant 4$ | 3 |
| $4 < m \leqslant 5$ | 2 |
| $5 < m$ | 3 |

Based on these results, estimate the probability that her train is more than three minutes late.

# Problem

## *Odd socks!*

Both Ruth and Tim often have to get dressed in the dark so that they don't disturb the sister or brother who shares their bedroom.

Ruth has 6 blue socks and 8 white socks in her drawer. How many socks will she need to get out if she want to be sure of getting two of the same colour?

Tim has 6 red socks, 8 green socks and 4 blue socks. He always likes to wear socks which do not match! What is the smallest number of socks he will need to get out to be satisfied?

*Problem No 49*

# Solution

## *Odd socks*

Ruth only need to get three socks out. Even if the first two are different, the third will match one of the first two.

Tim will need to get out nine socks just in case all the first eight are green.

---

Both Ruth and Tim often have to get dressed in the dark so that they don't disturb the sister or brother who shares their bedroom.

Ruth has 6 blue socks and 8 white socks in her drawer. How many socks will she need to get out if she want to be sure of getting two of the same colour?

Tim has 6 red socks, 8 green socks and 4 blue socks. He always likes to wear socks which do not match! What is the smallest number of socks he will need to get out to be satisfied?

---

*Solution No 49*

# Problem

*Cars*

A survey has been carried out in the office car park and it has been seen that one tenth of the cars are blue and that half are more than three years old.

Estimate the probability that the next car to drive out of the car park is both blue and over three years old.

# Solution

## *Cars*

In this case the two probabilities simply need to be multiplied so the probability is $\dfrac{1}{10} \times \dfrac{1}{2} = \dfrac{1}{20} = 0.05$.

A survey has been carried out in the office car park and it has been seen that one tenth of the cars are blue and that half are more than three years old.

Estimate the probability that the next car to drive out of the car park is both blue and over three years old.

# Problem

*A square triangle!*

Can you draw a triangle in such a way that all the angles, measured in degrees, are square numbers?

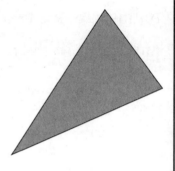

Can you do the same for a quadrilateral?

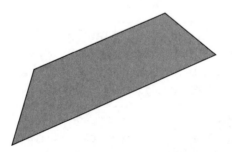

# Solution

## A square triangle!

You need three square numbers which add up to 180. A possible solution to the triangle is for the angles to be 100°, 64° and 16°.  *(Can you find any more?)*

You need four square numbers which add up to 360. Possible solutions are 4°, 36°, 64° and 256° or 196°, 144°, 16° and 4°.

Can you draw a triangle in such a way that all the angles, measured in degrees, are square numbers?

Can you do the same for a quadrilateral?

*Solution No 51*

# Problem

## *A dicey question*

George the gambler is always looking for new ways to try to muddle his opponents. This time he is playing a simple game with two dice but, instead of betting on the score shown by adding the two top numbers, he has decided to bet on the score worked out by adding all ten of the numbers which can be seen.

Which is the best number for you to bet on to beat George at his game?

# Solution

## *A dicey question*

Bet on **35** to have the best chance of winning.

As there are only two faces of the dice hidden, the most likely total which is hidden is 7. (Can you explain why?) The total of the two dice comes to 42 (21 for each of them) so it is best to bet on 42 – 7.

---

George the gambler is always looking for new ways to try to muddle his opponents. This time he is playing a simple game with two dice but, instead of betting on the score shown by adding the two top numbers, he has decided to bet on the score worked out by adding all ten of the numbers which can be seen.

Which is the best number for you to bet on to beat George at his game?

---

*Solution No 52*

# Problem

## *A postal problem*

Mrs Brown is getting rather absent minded.  Last week she wrote six letters and addressed six envelopes  but she didn't put the all letters into the right envelopes!

How many different ways could she do this  so that four of the letters were actually right?

Could she have got exactly five of them right?

# Solution

## *A postal problem*

### She could get four right in 15 ways.

There are six envelopes which one 'wrong' letter can go into and that 'wrong' letter can be any one of five. Then the other 'wrong' envelope must contain the 'wrong' letter left over for the other four to be correct. However, the same outcome would have occurred if these had been done in the reverse order so, each wrong solution has been counted twice. Thus the answer is $6 \times 5 \div 2 = 15$.

### There is **no** way that she can get exactly five letters right.

If five are right, the sixth has only one letter to go into one envelope which must be the correct one.

---

Mrs Brown is getting rather absent minded. Last week she wrote six letters and addressed six envelopes but she didn't put the letters into the right envelopes!

How many different ways could she do this so that four of the letters were actually right?
Could she have got exactly five of them right?

---

*Solution No 53*

# Problem

## *Dice with a difference*

A tetrahedral die (dice) is made using four equilateral triangles. The faces are numbered 1 to 4. The score when the die is thrown is defined as the number on the face which is on the table, i.e. hidden.

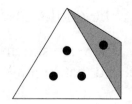

Two of these dice are thrown and their scores are **subtracted**, always taking the smaller number, if there is one, from the larger.

What is the most likely score?

*Problem No 54*

# Solution

## *Dice with a difference*

The most likely score is **1**, as can be seen from the difference table below:

| Score on dice | 1 | 2 | 3 | 4 |
|---|---|---|---|---|
| 1 | 0 | 1 | 2 | 3 |
| 2 | 1 | 0 | 1 | 2 |
| 3 | 2 | 1 | 0 | 1 |
| 4 | 3 | 2 | 1 | 0 |

You could use a similar method to look at the sums or products of the two scores.

A tetrahedral die (dice) is made using four equilateral triangles. The faces are numbered 1 to 4. The score when the die is thrown is defined as the number on the face which is on the table, i.e. hidden.

Two of these dice are thrown and their scores are subtracted, always taking the smaller number, if there is one, from the larger.

What is the most likely score?

*Solution No 54*

# Problem

*A prime problem*

Which numbers, less than 100, are the product of exactly three *different* prime factors?

# Solution

### *A prime problem*

The only numbers are:

$$30 = 2 \times 3 \times 5$$
$$42 = 2 \times 3 \times 7$$
$$66 = 2 \times 3 \times 11$$
$$70 = 2 \times 5 \times 7$$

and
$$78 = 2 \times 3 \times 13.$$

(Rather than searching through the numbers up to 100, look at the first few prime numbers and their products.)

---

Which numbers, less than 100, are the product of exactly three different prime factors?

---

# Problem

## *Bowling Alley*

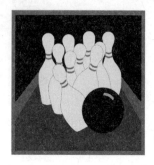

In her last game, Mary bowled 199 and this effort raised her average from 177 to 178.

To raise her average to 179 with the next game, what must she bowl?

# Solution

## *Bowling Alley*

She needs to bowl **201**.

Suppose Mary has now bowled $n$ times, she has scored a total of $178n$. Before this she had bowled $n - 1$ times, a total of $177(n - 1)$. So

$$177(n - 1) + 199 = 178n$$

which solves to give

$$n = 22.$$

After the next game she will have bowled 23 times and needs to achieve a total of $23 \times 179 = 4117$.

Her previous total was $22 \times 178 = 3916$ so she needs to bowl $4117 - 3916 = 201$ with her next game.

---

In her last game, Mary bowled 199 and this effort raised her average from 177 to 178.
To raise her average to 179 with the next game, what must she bowl?

# Problem

## *A mean question!*

I am thinking of five numbers.

The mean of these numbers is 4, the median is 3, the mode is 1 and the range is 9.

What are my five numbers?

# Solution

## *A mean question!*

The numbers are **1, 1, 3, 5, 10**.

The mode and median lead to the first two numbers both being 1 and the third (central) number being 3. The range gives the largest as 10 and the mean gives the total as 20.

---

I am thinking of five numbers.

The mean of these numbers is 4, the median is 3, the mode is 1 and the range is 9.

What are my five numbers?

---

# Problem

## *Work this one out*

Choose any three-digit number whose digits are all different. Carry out the following steps:

A)   Reverse this number to give a second number.
B)   Take the smaller of these two numbers from the larger.

Now add this number to the number obtained by reversing its digits. What do you get?

Try again starting with a different three digit number.

Is your answer always going to be the same?

Explain.

# Solution

## *Work this one out*

The answer should always come to **1089.**

Suppose the three digit number is *cba* where *c*     $c\ b\ a$
is bigger than *a*. When we write the reversed     $-\ a\ b\ c$
number underneath we need to borrow from
the tens and also the hundreds so that we can take *c* from *a* in
the units column leading to $c - a - 1$ in the first column, 9
in the second and $10 + a - c$ in the third.

The value of this number is:

$$100(c - a - 1) + 90 + 10 + a - c.$$

When this number is reversed its value becomes:

$$100(10 + a - c) + 90 + 10 + (c - a - 1).$$

Simplifying each of these gives $99c - 99a$ and
$1089 - 99c + 99a$ so, the result when we add is 1089.

---

Choose any three-digit number whose digits are all different.
Carry out the following steps:

A)     Reverse this number to give a second number.

B)     Take the smaller of these two numbers from the larger.

Now add this number to the number obtained by reversing its
digits. What do you get?

Try again starting with a different three digit number.

Is your answer always going to be the same? Explain.

---

*Solution No 58*

# Problem

## *The tournament*

If there are sixteen players in a knockout tournament, how many games will be played in total to find a winner?

How many games would be needed if there were 20 players at first, some of whom would get a 'bye' in the first round and proceed straight to the second round?

Can you find a general rule?

*Problem No 59*

# Solution

## *The tournament*

There will be **15** games (8 in the first round, 4 in the second, 2 in the third and one in the last).

With 20 players, there must be **19** games.

The general rule is that $n$ players need $n - 1$ games.
(Each game knocks out one player so there must always be one less games than the number of players at the start.)

---

If there are sixteen players in a knockout tournament, how many games will be played in total to find a winner?

How many games would be needed if there were 20 players at first, some of whom would get a 'bye' in the first round and proceed straight to the second round?

Can you find a general rule?

---

# Problem

## *Balancing Act*

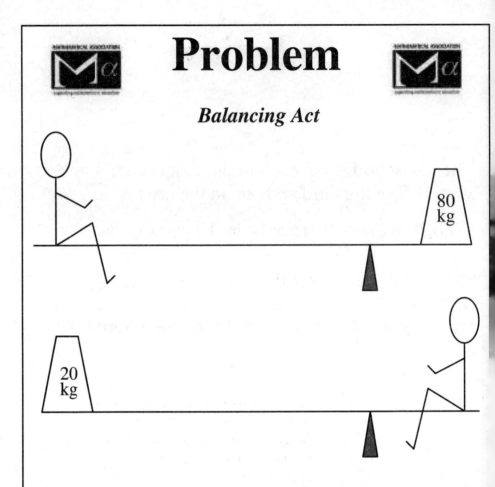

If Joe balances the see-saw with an 80 kg box, as shown in the first diagram, then switches ends and balances the see-saw with an 20 kg box, as shown in the second diagram.

How much does Joe weigh?

*Problem No 60*

# Solution

## *Balancing Act*

Joe weighs **40 kg**.

If Joe weighs $m$ kg, the distance on the left is $x$ cm and the distance on the right is $y$ cm then the following equations can be formed:

$$mx = 80y$$
$$20x = my.$$

As neither $x$ nor $y$ is zero, we can divide one equation by the other to get

$$\frac{m}{20} = \frac{80}{m},$$

leading to $m^2 = 1600$. So $m = 40$.

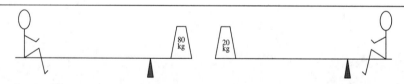

If Joe balances the see-saw with an 80 kg box, as shown in the first diagram, then switches ends and balances the see-saw with an 20 kg box, as shown in the second diagram.
How much does Joe weigh?

*Solution No 60*

# Problem

## *Washing the dishes*

After an *enormous* party there are 150 items to be washed up by hand.
John says he can do it in 50 minutes. James knows that he is slower and would take 1¼ hours.

They decide to do it together. How long will they take and how will they go about it?

*Problem No 61*

# Solution

## *Washing the dishes*

They can do it in **30 minutes**.

John washes 3 items in a minute and James washes 2 so, between them they can wash 5 a minute.

Eventually, John will have washed 90 of them and James 60.

(N.B. This assumes that there are two sinks!)

---

After an *enormous* party there are 150 items to be washed up by hand.

John says he can do it in 50 minutes. James knows that he is slower and would take 1¼ hours.

They decide to do it together. How long will they take and how will they go about it?

---

# Problem

## *Lock it up*

Sam has been given a new game which has a simple combination lock on it. There are four dials, each having the numbers 1, 2, 3 and 4.

At first, Sam decides that each number of the combination will be different.

In how many ways can this be done? If all these combinations were written down and added, what would the total be? (Look for a quick method.)

What would your answers be if each number could be used more than once in a combination?

# Solution

## *Lock it up*

If each number is used only once, there are **24** different combinations totalling **240.**

(There are 4 choices for the first digit, then 3 for the second, 2 for the third and only 1 for the last giving 24 in all. Each combination adds to 10 so the total is 240.)

If repetitions are allowed there are **256** combinations, adding to **2560.**

(Now there are 4 choices for each digit so the number of combinations is 4 × 4 × 4 × 4.

Each digit will have been used the same number of times, i.e. 256 so we can multiply by 10 again.)

---

Sam has been given a new game which has a simple combination lock on it. There are four dials, each having the numbers 1, 2, 3 and 4.

At first, Sam decides that each number of the combination will be different.

In how many ways can this be done? If all these combinations were written down and added, what would the total be? (Look for a quick method.)

What would your answers be if each number could be used more than once in a combination?

---

*Solution No 62*

# Problem

## *Broom Handles*

A shop sells handles for garden brooms which are made up of cylinders of wood, diameter 5 centimetres.

I bought three of these and, to keep them together, put a rubber band round each end of the bundle.   How long will each rubber band be?

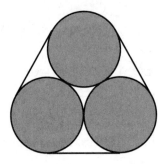

*Problem No 63*

# Solution

## *Broom Handles*

Each rubber band is **(15 + 5π)** ≈ **30.7 cm** (3 s. f.) long.

(If you look at the diagram you will see that the band is made up of three straight sections, each the same length as the diameter, 5 cm, and three curved sections, each a third of a circle making a complete circle of diameter 5 cm i.e. 5π cm.)

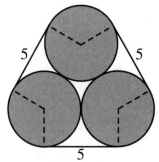

A shop sells handles for garden brooms which are made up of cylinders of wood, diameter 5 centimetres.

I bought three of these and, to keep them together, put a rubber band round each end of the bundle. How long will each rubber band be?

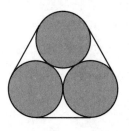

*Solution No 63*

# Problem

## *The hill*

A cyclist enjoys riding to the top of a hill near his house and then down again, knowing that the length of the hill is exactly one mile up and, of course, one mile down again.

He aims to do the whole trip at an average speed of 15 mph.

If he can climb the hill at an average speed of 10 mph, how fast will he need to come down again?

Having perfected this, he decides to go even faster on the journey down, even though he knows that 10 mph is the best he can do uphill, so that his average overall is now 20 mph. How fast must he come down now?

# Solution

## *The hill*

He needs to come down at **30 mph**.
(To average 15 mph over the 2 miles he needs to take a total of 8 minutes. 1 mile at 10 mph takes 6 minutes so he needs to come down in 2 minutes, 30 mph.)

It is **impossible** to average 20 mph.
(As before, he takes 6 minutes to climb the hill but, to do 2 miles at an average of 20 mph, he needs to take 6 minutes over the whole journey so has no time at all to get down again.)

---

A cyclist enjoys riding to the top of a hill near his house and then down again, knowing that the length of the hill is exactly one mile up and, of course, one mile down again.

He aims to do the whole trip at an average speed of 15 mph.

If he can climb the hill at an average speed of 10 mph, how fast will he need to come down again?

Having perfected this, he decides to go even faster on the journey down, even though he knows that 10 mph is the best he can do uphill, so that his average overall is now 20 mph. How fast must he come down now?

---